W9-AJP-195

How to Make (and Keep) Friends

SMART TALK

How to Make (and Keep) Friends

Elizabeth Karlsberg

Troll Associates

ACKNOWLEDGEMENT

A special thanks to Richard A. Reinhart, Ph.D., Chief Psychologist, Ventura County California Mental Health, whose expertise proved invaluable in writing this book.

Library of Congress Cataloging-in-Publication Data

Karlsberg, Elizabeth.
   How to make (and keep) friends / by Elizabeth Karlsberg;
illustrated by Diana Magnuson.
     p.   cm.—(Smart talk)
   Summary: A guide for girls on how to deal with cliques, patch up
arguments, and keep friendships going strong.
   ISBN 0-8167-2295-1 (lib. bdg.)   ISBN 0-8167-2296-X (pbk.)
   1. Friendship--Juvenile literature. 2. Girls—Conduct of life.
[1. Friendship.] I. Magnuson, Diana, ill. II. Title.
III. Series.
B575.F66K37 1991
158'.25—dc20   90-48252

Copyright © 1991 by Troll Associates

All rights reserved. No part of this book may be used or reproduced in any manner whatsoever without written permission from the publisher.
Printed in the United States of America.
10 9 8 7 6 5 4 3

Friends and
Friendship

*F*riends. Can you imagine what life would be like without them? Who would you hang out with in the cafeteria during lunch? Who would you tell about the new boy in your history class who's both cute *and* smart? Who would you turn to if you tried out for cheerleading—again—and still didn't make the squad? Who would you have those marathon phone conversations with—you know, the ones that drive your parents crazy?

Let's face it. Without friends, the world would be a pretty lonely place. Although friends and friendship mean different things to different people, most people realize that friends are pretty important. Just how important, you ask? So important that poets, philosophers—even presidents—have written volumes on the subject of friendship.

While it's fun to read what other people have said about friendship, what matters is what *you* think of when you hear the word "friend." Your own personal definition of friendship has a lot to do with the kind of friend you are. If, for instance, you believe that the quality of loyalty goes hand in hand with friendship, you're probably a loyal friend yourself. If you believe a friend is someone who'll go out of her way for you, maybe just to pick up a homework assignment you missed when you were sick, it's likely that you'd also go out of your way for your friends.

FROM FAMILY TO FRIENDS

Friends take on a special significance about the time that you become a teen. When you were a child, you most likely looked to your mom or dad for the support you needed and to answer any questions you had. Although you may have had disagreements with your parents at times, their ideas probably matched up with yours quite nicely, or rather, yours matched up with theirs. Part of growing up involves learning to form ideas and opinions of your own.

As you go about the process of discovering the kind of person you are and what you want to be, it's only natural that you look to your friends more than your parents for similarities in feelings. Your friends are making the same discoveries you are. They may also be facing the same kinds of problems—from peer pressure to sibling squabbles. Naturally, you feel that your friends are in a better position than your parents to understand you. Or, as Helen puts it, "Sure, your parents were your age once, but that was decades ago. Besides, times have changed." (Actually, your parents probably understand you better than you think, but we'll go into that later.)

Friends play a vital role in your life. They help you make the shift from complete dependence on your parents to independence. In a very real sense, you and your friends are preparing for your future as adults when you'll be interacting more frequently with people outside of your family.

FRIENDSHIP IS GOOD FOR YOU

Are you surprised to learn that your friends, in a roundabout way, are helping you to prepare for your future? There are plenty of other fabulous fringe benefits to friendship as well. You know that good feeling you get when you unexpectedly run into a friend? Not only can it make you smile and laugh with pleasure, but there's scientific proof that friendship is good for your health. No joke! Studies show that our bodies actually benefit from the presence of friends. Blood pressure drops, stomach acids are reduced, even the heart rate slows to a more relaxed pace. All this translates into one thing: a healthier you. Not bad, huh?

FINDING FRIENDSHIP

It's not only your body that gets a boost from friendship. What it does for a person's spirits is simply amazing. Have you ever received a birthday card or note from somebody who signs it "Love, your friend . . ."? Somehow that little extra touch, a declaration of your friendship, makes you feel special. It says "you matter" and "I care about you," as well as a bunch of other nice things that make you feel appreciated.

Because of all the wonderful things friendship can do, it's no surprise that we all crave it. Look at it like this: How long could you go without talking to your friends? It's a good guess that without your daily dose of friendship, you just wouldn't be the same, happy you.

There's just one problem. Despite what many people think, friendship isn't always easy. Some days, the friend you have the most fun with can turn out to be the one who frustrates you the most. Also, good friendships certainly don't grow on trees. Like a young tree, though, a friendship needs careful nurturing if it is to develop deep roots and grow strong.

Like any relationship, a friendship can be fragile.

It takes practice to master the art. That's why if you begin being a good friend immediately, not only will you make the most of your friendships now, but you'll also be surrounded by faithful friends forever.

Becoming a Friend

*H*ave you ever asked yourself what kind of friend *you* are? Chances are, you're interested in being the best kind of friend you can be. But as you're about to see, friendship demands many things, the first of which is that it cannot be taken for granted.

Even someone who's a good friend already can learn to be an even better one. The following "friendly" quiz can help you determine your areas of strength and weakness as a friend. Don't worry: This isn't meant to be a true indicator of what kind of friend you *are*, but rather a guide to the kind of friend you can *become*.

For all quizzes, please write your answers on a separate piece of paper.

☆☆ A "FRIENDLY" QUIZ ☆☆

1. *A friend of yours just got her hair cut in a not very flattering style—and she knows it. Still, after complaining, she asks you for your opinion. You say:*
   a. "It looks wonderful!" (You don't want to make her feel bad.)
   b. "Who did this to you? You must be devastated."
   c. "I think I liked your old cut better too, but it'll grow out in no time."
2. *You notice a new girl in school sitting by herself at lunch. You're sitting with your friends, and don't know anything about her except that she's new. You:*
   a. Immediately go over, ask her to sit at your table and offer to introduce her to your friends.
   b. Point her out to your friends, so that they all turn to look in her direction.
   c. Aren't sure how your friends will react, so you wait until later to talk to her.
3. *One of your good friends has done something that really hurt your feelings. You:*
   a. Give her the cold shoulder until she asks what's wrong.
   b. Talk to her about what happened and explain why you're hurt.

   c. Try to forget about it; you don't want to risk ruining your friendship.

4. *You want to ask Greg to a school dance but find out that a friend of yours is also planning on inviting him. You:*
   a. Hurry up and ask him before she gets the chance to.
   b. Wait until you can talk to her, so you can both decide what to do.
   c. Decide not to ask him.

5. *You meet a girl you really like, but are afraid she wouldn't fit in with your group. You:*
   a. Decide to pursue her friendship anyway, even if your other friends don't approve.
   b. See her on a one-on-one basis only—so your group doesn't have to know.
   c. Decide not to risk becoming her friend since it might mean the group would abandon you.

6. *A friend of yours confesses that she doesn't feel prepared for an important exam and asks you to feed her the answers during the test. You:*
   a. Agree to help her out; after all, she's your friend.
   b. Refuse, knowing that it might end your friendship.
   c. Tell her that you're afraid cheating could get you into trouble, but give in anyway when she pushes.

7. *You notice that a friend of yours has been acting depressed, and you don't know why. You:*
   a. Let her know you're there for her if she wants to talk.

9

b. Tell her to snap out of it; things will get better.

c. Don't worry about it. She's probably just going through a phase and she'll talk to you when she needs to.

8. *A friend of yours has been acting more and more possessive, and gets upset anytime you see another friend. You*:

a. Decide it's easier to include her than have her angry at you.

b. Purposely exclude her from all future plans until she gets the hint.

c. Assure her that you value your friendship with her, but that your other friendships are also important to you.

Scoring: Give yourself the proper number of points for each answer you chose. Then total them up to see how you'll fare in friendship.

1) a. 1	2) a. 2	3) a. 0	4) a. 0
b. 0	b. 0	b. 2	b. 2
c. 2	c. 1	c. 1	c. 1

5) a. 2	6) a. 0	7) a. 2	8) a. 1
b. 1	b. 2	b. 0	b. 0
c. 0	c. 0	c. 1	c. 2

If you scored:

11–16 points: You're a true-blue friend. It's no wonder you're surrounded by a loyal group of pals. You've obviously mastered some of the finer friendship techniques. Keep up the good work.

5–10 points: In your desire to be a good friend—

and you usually are one—you may be overlooking somebody important: yourself. You matter too, and your real friends will respect you for standing up for yourself.

0–4 points: It's okay to expect a lot from your friends, but you've also got to be willing to give the same in return. Holding grudges or going along with the gang when you really don't want to won't build stronger friendships. It may cause them to self-destruct. Don't be afraid to speak your mind: Your *real* friends will listen.

☆☆☆

BEYOND EXCUSES

It can happen almost anywhere: at school, at a party, at church or synagogue, at a sporting event. You notice someone—it might be a girl or a guy—and think, "I'd really like to meet that person," but because you don't know what to do or say, you don't. Or, maybe you do meet somebody—briefly—but that's as far as it goes, because you don't know how to let the person know that you'd like to be friends.

For Jenny, situations like these used to come up all too frequently. "Once, this new girl named Diana came to my school," Jenny said. "Just from observing her, I thought the two of us might hit it off. But because I didn't have the guts to ever say more than 'Hi' to her, we never got to know each other. I guess I was just too shy to say anything else."

Many friendships never get off the ground because of excuses like, "I'm just too shy." People make up all sorts of excuses to justify why certain friendships pass them by. Ask yourself this question: How many times have you let a potential friendship slip through your fingers?

PUTTING YOURSELF ON THE LINE

"She (or he) won't like me anyway, so why should I try?"

"It's not worth the effort."

"Nothing will come of it anyway."

Maybe one of the lines above sounds familiar to you. Maybe all of them do. Then again, you may be one of those lucky people who has never felt the least bit awkward about going right up to someone you want to know and telling them so. But at least once in our lives, most of us have muttered an excuse or two to ourselves for not befriending someone we wanted to get to know.

What's really behind all the excuses? We're afraid of being rejected—plain and simple. We convince ourselves that if we make an overture of friendship and it isn't accepted, we'll feel worse than if we hadn't ever tried, so we don't. That's how powerful the fear of rejection can be.

The end result? Many potential friendships go unexplored. It's true that if you don't put yourself on the line, you can't experience rejection. But you certainly won't experience lots of good things, either, such as all the special moments you could be sharing with a newfound friend.

Unfortunately, the fear of rejection tends to magnify any of the worries that you might have about yourself, which makes it even tougher to put yourself on the line. These worries can take many different forms. You might find yourself asking questions like: "Am I interesting enough to be this person's friend?" "What do I have to offer her?" "Does she think I dress okay?"

Most often, you're the only one who notices the things you spend so much time worrying about because people tend to focus on themselves. Chances are the person you want to know better has a whole slew of her own worries, and is too busy thinking about them to even notice the things you are so concerned about.

SHYNESS: THE NUMBER ONE HURDLE TO OVERCOME

Shyness is a very real obstacle to making new friends. That's the bad news. The *good* news is that shyness is *normal*. One study estimates that approximately 84 million Americans consider themselves shy. More good news: Most people aren't shy twenty-four hours a day, seven days a week. In other words, shyness comes and goes, and different situations cause different people to be shy. In fact, if you give it some thought, you'll probably realize that you only become shy in a few situations. Unfortunately, for many girls your age, shyness seems to strike at the worst possible moments—like when you see a gorgeous guy walking your way.

Once you overcome your shyness, it's easy to make new friends.

TAKING THE FIRST STEPS

The first step to overcoming shyness is to identify the situations that make you feel shy. Do you dread having to stand up in front of the class and deliver an oral report? Do you get nervous when you're alone with someone you don't know too well? Do you get tongue-tied any time a teacher calls on you?

Make a list of your own personal "shy situations." Sometimes just rehearsing what you'd do or say the next time the situation arises can make you feel more confident. If, for example, you can never think of anything to say to a particular person, plan ahead. That might mean preparing an "opening statement" you feel comfortable with. Or it might mean deciding on a list of possible things to talk about.

If this is difficult, try thinking about what you'd do in each situation if you *weren't* shy. How would you act? What would you say? The idea here is to practice not being shy in those situations until, finally, you no longer feel shy when they occur.

In general, it is a good idea to focus on the other person as much as possible. When you take your mind off yourself, you become less self-conscious, which automatically makes you less shy. So, listen to what the people talking to you are saying, notice their clothes or how they move their hands when they speak; all these details will keep you from feeling shy.

Another thing that can help you overcome your shyness is to develop a skill, quality or knowledge of something that you can bring up in a social situation:

- ❂ *Find your funny bone. Almost everyone appreciates someone who really knows how to tell a good joke.*
- ❂ *Become an authority on something. If you're into a certain kind of music, keep track of which bands are doing what and who's playing concerts when. If you're a film buff, find out all you can about movie stars and film history. This way you'll always have something to talk about and will never be at a loss for words.*
- ❂ *Develop a talent. If you play the piano or any other instrument, memorize a few pieces you could "perform" spontaneously at a party. Become a great dancer. No one has to know you practice in front of your mirror every night.*

An added benefit of these tricks is that knowing you are good at something, whatever it is, can do a lot to boost your confidence—and that, too, can help you to shed your shyness.

WHAT'S ALL THIS STUFF ABOUT SELF-ESTEEM?

You've heard the phrase a hundred times: *self-esteem*. It's something parents, teachers and school counselors often talk about. And there's no more appropriate place to discuss it than in a book about friendship.

Self-esteem has to do with feeling good about

16

yourself. Some of you might wonder if you can have too much self-esteem. No, but you can be *conceited*, and a lot of people get the two concepts mixed up.

☆☆ WHICH IS WHICH QUIZ ☆☆

Do you know the difference between self-esteem and conceit? Take the following quiz to find out. Which word (self-esteem or conceit) would you associate with the following people and their actions? On a separate piece of paper, write "SE" (for self-esteem) or "C" (for conceit) after the number of each description:

1. *A girl tells you she* knows *she'll be nominated for Most Popular Student this year.*

2. *A popular guy introduces himself to a new boy in your class and offers to show him around the school.*

3. *A student raises his hand to answer* all *the teacher's questions so everyone will know how smart he is.*

4. *A classmate decides to run for student body president because she thinks she can make a difference.*

5. *A basketball player who scored 30 points in last night's game makes sure everybody knows about it.*

6. *A friend applies for an important academic honor—and wins—but you don't find out until it's announced in the school paper.*

7. *A girl is elected photo editor of the school yearbook, and splashes photos of herself throughout it.*

Answers: 1. C; 2. SE; 3. C; 4. SE; 5. C; 6. SE; 7. C.

☆☆☆

If you were confused by some of the answers it's because both self-esteem and conceit have something to do with confidence. So what's the difference between the two words? Webster's Dictionary defines self-esteem as "a confidence and satisfaction in oneself." Conceit, on the other hand, is an "excessive appreciation of one's own worth," and being conceited is "having an excessively high opinion of oneself."

The word "excessive" is the key. Believe it or not, the people who seem the most conceited are often the ones who are most lacking in self-esteem. To illustrate using some of the examples from the quiz, only someone who's very insecure needs to *prove* he's smart. The girl who has a burning need to tell you she "knows she's going to be nominated for Most Popular Student" might come across as unusually confident. Then again, she also needs your attention and approval, and that means she's really not as self-assured as she appears to be.

In contrast, there's absolutely nothing wrong with having a sense of your own worth. A healthy measure of self-esteem can give you the courage to pursue difficult challenges, enable you to stand up

18

for yourself and allow you to overcome any fears you might have about forming new friendships. It makes you feel good about yourself, and feeling good about yourself lets you feel comfortable with yourself. People who are comfortable with themselves make the people around them feel comfortable; so, in a roundabout way, your self-esteem puts other people at ease. That's why it's so important to friendship.

YOU WANT TO BE FRIENDS WITH ME?

What else does self-esteem have to do with friendship? For starters, the more self-esteem you have, the more you feel you have to offer a new friend. While someone who doesn't think very highly of herself might think, "Why would this person want to be friends with me?" the answer to that question would be obvious to someone more self-assured.

But no matter how much self-esteem you have, you're still going to be vulnerable. Self-esteem won't make you immune to rejection. No one is. When you reach out for a person's friendship, it's as if you're saying, "Hey, this is me. This is what I'm like. So, what do you think? Can we be friends?" If you are rebuffed—ouch!—it's going to hurt, no matter what. Self-esteem won't ensure that your feelings will never be hurt. However, it can help to make that hurt heal more quickly because you know that even though one person doesn't want to be your friend, you're still worth being friends with. That knowledge will give you the confidence to go out there and make friends!

A Foolproof Recipe for Friendship

*A*ha! Here it is at last, the secret recipe for friendship success. Just add a dash of this, a generous helping of that, maybe a smidgen of something else and—voilà!—just like that, you've whipped up a sensational friendship soufflé.

Hey, not so fast. It's true that without a few key ingredients, most friendships would flop. But when it comes to creating a special bond between two people, there's more than one way to make a masterpiece.

DIFFERENT PEOPLE, DIFFERENT APPROACHES

Take Tanya, for example. All her friends adore her. She's a bundle of energy from the moment she wakes up until the second she goes to sleep. Tanya can be a little on the loud side—you can hear her coming *long* before she walks into a room—but that doesn't bother her friends one bit. They think she's incredibly fun. At the same time, they know that if they ever needed to ask Tanya a serious question, she'd give them a no-nonsense answer. Tanya is one girl who doesn't beat around the bush about anything, especially not when it concerns her friends.

In contrast to Tanya's frenzied kind of friendship, Gail takes a quieter approach. Though she's as well-liked as Tanya, Gail prefers the company of just one or two friends at a time. People who don't know Gail well often mistake her sensitive, soft-spoken nature for shyness or as a sign that she has little to say. Nothing could be further from the truth: Gail can be a real motormouth, it just takes her a while to feel completely at ease around people she doesn't know well. If somebody asks her for her opinion, Gail is careful about what she says and how she says it—something her friends appreciate.

Tanya and Gail are two completely different people, but they're both good friends. Each girl's unique "friendship approach" reflects the individual she is, and that's precisely why it works for her. It would be silly for Tanya to try to downplay her exuberant, enthusiastic nature. That's one of the things people like best about her. And why should Gail pretend to be someone she's not when so many people think she's terrific?

Again, this all relates to the idea of feeling comfortable enough with yourself to *be* yourself. Not only is it a lot harder to put on an act, or borrow a different personality, it's not an effective strategy when it comes to making and keeping friends. First, it's impossible to keep up such an act. Second, you won't feel good about keeping the *real* you hidden inside.

You say you don't think you have your own unique friendship flair? Nonsense; you simply may not have found it yet!

FINDING YOUR FRIENDSHIP FLAIR

This is an activity you can do either on your own or with one of your friends. If you do get together with someone else for this, take turns asking each other the following questions. Note: You might want to tape-record or write the answers down on a separate piece of paper so you can think about and learn from them.

FRIENDSHIP FLAIR QUESTIONNAIRE

1. When your friends have complimented you in the past, what kinds of things have they said? Think of as many examples as you can, and be specific.
2. If you were to give yourself three compliments, what would they be?
3. If you asked each of your friends what they thought the best thing about you was, what do you think they'd say? (Example: Linda would say the best thing about me is my sense of humor, Julie would say the best thing about me is my ability to put people at ease, Mary would say . . . and so on.)
4. Now, ask yourself the same question, and complete this sentence: "I think the best thing about me is ———." (Fill in the blank.)
5. As a friend, what would you say are your three best qualities?

After you've finished, consider your answers. Is there a similar pattern between how you see yourself and how you believe your friends see you? If so, you do a good job of presenting an accurate picture of yourself to your pals, and you've probably pinpointed your friendship flair. If, on the other hand, there's a distinct difference between what you and your friends see, then one of two things may be true: a) The qualities you feel are your best aren't coming across loud and clear (ask yourself why), or b) You've got a multifaceted flair for friendship.

THE MUST-HAVES

Let's go back to our sensational friendship soufflé. Here's what you have to blend into the mixture if you want the finished product to be a hit:

HONESTY

How do you feel when you find out that a friend has lied to you? Pretty awful, huh? Probably one of the first thoughts that goes through your head is, "Didn't she think enough of me to tell me the truth?"

That's one of the big problems with lying: It calls into question everything you thought your friendship was based on. You feel that your friend doesn't *trust* you enough, isn't *comfortable* enough with you or doesn't even *like* you enough to be honest with you.

Usually though, lying has little to do with you, and a lot to do with how the person who lied feels about him or herself. Sometimes people who lie are afraid of what their friends would think of them if they told the truth. They might want to impress others. Or they might think the truth is so boring that they have to spice it up. Generally speaking, people who lie are afraid of the consequences telling the truth might bring. What these same people forget is that dishonesty usually brings much tougher consequences.

Let's say your friend Susan tells you she has to baby-sit her little brother, so she won't be able to go shopping with you. Later that day, you just happen to run into her at an ice cream shop with one of your mutual friends. Susan squirms in embarrassment when she sees you, knowing that she's just been caught in a lie. She tries to explain: "I thought you'd be angry that we didn't include you."

"I thought you'd be angry . . ." is one of the most common excuses people use to explain their lies. Variations of it include: "I didn't want to hurt your feelings," "I thought that you wouldn't understand" and so on. Yes, chances are that if your friend had told the truth, you might have been angry, hurt or confused. But that doesn't make it okay for her to lie to you.

Someone who truly cares about another person's feelings doesn't lie to that person. Anger, hurt and misunderstandings . . . these are all problems that most of us can work through. It's much more difficult to rebuild trust once it's been destroyed by dishonesty.

An "honest" friendship survives anger, hurt and misunderstandings. Why? Because along with honesty comes security, the feeling two friends share when they know they can always depend on each other to tell the truth.

COMMUNICATION
PART ONE: TALKING

When a problem arises, good communication skills can come in especially handy. Many teens don't like to express certain feelings to their friends,

Good communication means not only being a good talker,
but being a caring listener.

especially if those feelings involve anger. You know how that is: You're afraid that if you get upset with your friend, you'll "blow" the friendship. Not so! If you're angry at your friend and *don't* say anything, *then* you'll almost certainly blow it. In fact, this is a perfect opportunity to deepen your friendship. By talking out your problems, the two of you can strengthen the closeness you already feel. Besides, if your friend doesn't know something is wrong, how can she make it right?

And remember, in a friendship, it's equally important to air *good* feelings, not just complaints. When a friend is helpful, or does something nice for you, tell her how much you appreciate it. (One last tip: Your friend may know she means a lot to you, but if you mention it to her every so often, both of you will feel even better.)

COMMUNICATION
PART TWO: LISTENING

You might think that because you speak or write well, you're a good communicator. Well, you're half right. Being able to express yourself is important to good communication, but it's only part of the picture. Communication is a two-way process.

The best communicators may be good "expressers," but they are even better listeners. The problem is that many people don't really know how to listen. You'd think it'd be easy enough to do, but lots of things get in the way. The most important thing to keep in mind is that listening means *listen-*

ing, not thinking of what you're going to say next, not giving advice. Just listening. So, if someone asks you to listen to them, it is your job to sit quietly and let them use you as a sounding board against which they can work out their own ideas. And then if you need someone to listen to you, you can expect the same treatment.

Remember, you spend years in school trying to perfect your speech and writing, but you've probably never had listening lessons in your life. Like anything else you want to be good at, listening takes practice. Luckily, it's never too late to learn.

LOYALTY

Nothing solidifies a friendship like loyalty, and nothing can break it apart faster than a breach of that loyalty. Faithful friends not only stand by each other, they stand up for each other. A loyal friend will come to your defense the moment someone puts you down. She's a constant source of support and strength. Finally, a loyal friend is reliable: You can depend on her to tell you the truth, and to be true to you.

SHARING

Friendship is built on shared experiences. When you share something with a friend, or when she shares something with you, the two of you are piecing together your friendship history. Sharing is what initially draws you closer together and, even-

29

tually, it's the wealth of your shared experiences that will help keep you close.

Whenever you share with someone else—your time, your belongings, your thoughts—you're offering that person a part of yourself. In a good friendship, the sharing goes both ways. There's a comfortable, easy exchange; no need for keeping score since both people receive as much as they give.

Think about a time when you did something nice for a friend. Maybe you sent her a "care" package at camp. Maybe you sat through a movie you didn't like because you knew how much she wanted to see it. You gave something to your friend, but you also got something back: the good feeling that came from making her happy. That's what giving and sharing are all about.

SECRETS AND OTHER SERIOUS STUFF

Friends share something else that's special: secrets. When you tell a friend a secret, you not only entrust her with a piece of privileged information, you in effect ask her to pledge her loyalty to you. That's why keeping a secret is a big deal; it's a sign that you're a trustworthy friend. But is it always the right thing to do? Maybe it's time to reconsider the sacred status of the secret.

Suppose someone approached you and asked you this question: "Would you ever fink on a friend?" What would your answer be? You would probably say a quick "no" without even thinking about it. Most girls think telling something entrusted to them as a secret is the worst thing one friend can do to another friend.

What if a friend swore you to secrecy, made you promise you wouldn't tell a soul, about something very important? Maybe she had started drinking alcohol, taking drugs or even talking about suicide. She made it clear that she didn't want anyone— especially her family—to find out. What would you do? Is this a case where it would actually be *okay* to tell?

YES! If you strongly disagree with this, ask yourself one very serious question: Wouldn't you rather have an angry friend than a sick or dead one? If you can save a person a lot of misery, or if you can even save a life, it's certainly worth letting the secret out of the bag.

Best Friends Forever

Sherry and Melissa, both bright and bubbly girls about your age, met years ago on the first day of kindergarten. They must have made a good first impression on each other because ever since that fateful day they've been practically inseparable.

As their friendship continued to blossom, Sherry and Melissa found they shared many interests, as best buddies often do. They're both crazy about clothes. They're French fry fanatics. They're nuts about any and all animals. They both love basketball, especially their hometown team. Most of all, each girl thinks the other is the greatest.

THAT SPECIAL BOND

There's no doubt that Sherry is Melissa's biggest fan, and Melissa is Sherry's. But the special bond that develops between best friends is not just about common interests, or even liking each other a lot. It's about being able to bare your soul knowing that you won't be laughed at. It's about the good times you both enjoy, and the bad times you help each other through. Most important, though, friendship is about bringing out the best in each other.

Melissa and Sherry both feel they're better people because of each other. That's one of the reasons their friendship, or any friendship for that matter, is such a big deal. Melissa and Sherry are both strong, capable girls, but they draw strength from each other as well. For example, one day in school, minutes before she was supposed to give an oral book report in front of their English class, Melissa suddenly panicked and drew a blank. Sherry noticed that her friend was in trouble so she quickly passed her a note of encouragement.

That did the trick. Thanks to Sherry's belief in her (and, of course, all the preparation she'd done in advance), Melissa gave one of her best book reports ever. After returning to her desk, she passed a note back to Sherry to thank her.

Of course, this was only one of the many times that Sherry has been there for Melissa. And there have been countless other times when Melissa has been Sherry's source of strength. Needless to say, when a friendship is this good, you want to do everything under the sun to keep it that way.

KEEP THE FRIENDSHIP FIRES BURNING

What's the best way to keep a friendship strong and steady? First, realize what the two of you have, and appreciate how good it really is.

When two people have been friends for a long time, they often start to take each other for granted. It's a problem even the best of friends face. Think about your closest friend for a moment. She's probably so much a part of you and you trust her so much that you just assume she'll always be there when you need her. This is one of the greatest things about having a best friend—but it's something both of you must protect.

It's not uncommon for long-term friendships to lose their fire every now and then. The spark that initially ignites the fun and laughter among friends may need refueling. In other words, you've got to feed the flames of friendship to keep them burning.

Sherry and Melissa never thought they could take each other for granted or that they could become bored. But all of a sudden both girls noticed that something had changed between them: They didn't laugh as much when they got together. Neither one really became very excited about plans they made. They argued about the silliest, smallest things. At first, Sherry and Melissa were afraid that their friendship was on the brink of collapse. They were facing something called "best-friend burnout" and they didn't know what to do.

Although it sounds pretty awful, best-friend burnout doesn't have to mean the end of a wonderful friendship. Before they dug themselves into a deeper hole, Melissa and Sherry decided to try to dig themselves out. They sat down and talked about what was going wrong, and how they could make it better. The two girls finally realized what the problem was: They weren't spending too much time together, they were spending too much time doing the *same old things* together. The result was that their friendship had become stuck in a rut.

How can you tell if you and your best friend are running your relationship into a rut? Start by asking yourselves the following questions:

☆☆ BURNOUT MINI-QUIZ ☆☆

1. *When my best friend and I make plans to get together outside of school, it's usually for the same activities.*
   True   False
2. *When the phone rings, and it's my best friend on the other line, I'm* _____ :
   a. Thrilled
   b. Indifferent
   c. Annoyed
3. *Lately, I seem to spend* _____ *of my time with my best friend.*
   a. All
   b. Very little
   c. About half

36

4. *Whenever I'm not with my best friend, I'm usually* _____ :
   a. Alone
   b. With another friend
   c. With my family
5. *Whenever I'm not with my best friend, she's usually* _____ :
   a. By herself
   b. With another one of her friends
   c. With her family
6. *The last time I did something really nice for my best friend was* _____ :
   a. Too long ago to remember
   b. Just the other day
   c. A while ago, but she still talks about it
7. *The last three or four times my best friend and I did something together, we both would agree that we had a good time.*
   True   False

There isn't a key for this quiz, because there are no right or wrong answers. You and your friend are the only ones who can evaluate the state of your friendship. If a trouble spot exists, the questions above can help you find it. But it will be up to the two of you to get yourselves back on track.

☆☆☆

37

SPICE IT UP!

If, like Sherry and Melissa, your friendship has fallen into a boring, predictable pattern, make a new plan of action. To spice up your time together, add some new choices to your friendship menu. If the two of you shop till you drop all the time, steer clear of the stores (at least for a while). If you mainly see movies together, go someplace where you'll be able to talk. Try activities neither of you have ever done before, or have never done *together*. Go bowling. Put on a pair of ice or roller skates. See what's new at the zoo. Take up tennis. How about horseback riding? The point is, resolve to do something *different*. It will make a big difference in your friendship.

Sometimes friendships fade because there are no surprises in them anymore. To liven things up a bit, plan an unexpected surprise for your friend. It doesn't have to be anything elaborate, just a small gesture to show her how much you care.

Think of what you might like someone to do for you. Your friend would probably appreciate the same kinds of things. You might give her flowers for no special occasion, or write her a simple "thanks-for-being-my-friend" note. If she always complains about having to exercise her dog, you might offer your dog-walking services for a day. Or offer to lend her that red sweater of yours she loves so much.

You don't have to spend lots of money to get your point across. Just use your imagination. One week-end, go over to her house and serve her a specially prepared "friendship feast" for breakfast. Or, "kidnap" her and take her to breakfast at your house. (For ideas like these, it's a good idea to ask your parents for help—and let hers in on it, too.) You'll probably come up with lots more great ideas. If you both work at it, your friendship can be even more fun than it was before!

THE TOO-TOGETHER TWOSOME

You probably can't imagine spending too much time with your best friend, right? It seems hard to believe, but if you and she want your times together to stay special, then you also need some time apart. There's nothing wrong with spending lots of time with your favorite friend. But going *everywhere* and doing *everything* together will eventually make you feel like a pair of Siamese twins.

You probably know friends like that, ones who might as well be joined at the hip. You never see one without the other. Sometimes, friends stick to each other like glue because they feel they need each other, kind of like a security blanket.

It's easy to understand why this happens. It's comforting to know that someone you trust, and who likes you for who you are, is by your side at all times. Unfortunately, this can not only prevent both of you from meeting new people, it can also keep you from growing as individuals. True, best friends should be able to depend on each other. But there's a difference between being able to depend on your best friend and being *dependent* on her.

Try new activities with old friends to add some spice to a tired friendship.

BREATHING ROOM

All friendships need breathing room. Without it they may eventually suffocate. Make no mistake: No one is suggesting that you and your friend should make a clean break from each other. Not at all! It may sound strange, but if you want to stay together as best friends for a long time, then you'll also have to make an effort to spend *some* time apart.

You might start by setting one day a week as your "apart" day. If that's too much, make it one day every two weeks. So you won't be left moping around the house or flipping TV channels every second, make plans ahead of time. Remember, though, just because you're apart neither of you has to be alone. If there's someone you've been wanting to get to know better, take the plunge. Call and invite her or him to spend some time with you. You may be surprised to find out how many people will be glad to hear from you.

WHEN CHANGE CHANGES YOUR FRIENDSHIP

Though a friendship sometimes starts to lose its steam because nothing is new, at other times best friends start drifting apart because something *has* changed. Maybe it's you who's changed. Maybe it's your friend. Or maybe it's both of you.

Even though best friends share many of the same

41

interests, they may develop different ones. Or they can grow apart because they're growing in opposite directions. That's what happened to Sally and Bonnie, who had been best friends for three years.

"The summer before ninth grade, Sally met some new kids," Bonnie remembered. "I'd been away at camp, and when I came back, she seemed really different. She just wasn't acting like the Sally I used to know. She'd started acting really 'tough.' I didn't think her new friends were all that great, but she did, I guess, and pretty soon she was spending more time with them than with me. When we did get together, it wasn't the same. I thought she had changed and she thought I had changed. Whatever happened, it altered our friendship for good."

When best friends start to go their separate ways, the transition isn't always smooth. It can be especially rough if your friend feels ready for something new and you don't. In fact, it can really hurt. But often, by the time one friend is ready for a change, the other is, too.

WHEN YOUR BEST FRIEND MAKES YOU BLUE

When your best friend does something that makes you mad, or hurts or just plain bugs you, it somehow feels much different—and worse—than if a "regular" friend had done the same thing. Why? Because she's your *best* friend so you automatically expect more from her.

Of course, this isn't fair. Even best friends can

blow it once in a while. Here's what to do when your best friend makes you blue:

- ✪ *Step One: Put yourself in her shoes.* Ask yourself, "What could she have been thinking of when she did this?" Sometimes that's all it takes for you to understand why she did what she did. It can also help to diminish your pain if you no longer feel she meant to make you unhappy.
- ✪ *Step Two: Discuss the problem with her.* Ask her about it and discuss what you both can do so the situation won't be a problem again.
- ✪ *Step Three: Make up.* There's nothing worse than being at odds with your best friend. Since she will probably feel bad for making you sad, reassure her that she is still your friend. She may know it already, but it's always nice to hear that someone thinks you're special— especially if that someone is your best friend. And if you do something that makes your best friend frown, put your pride aside and apologize.

Cliques:
The Friendship Barrier

Whether you hail from Anchorage, Alaska, Fort Lauderdale, Florida or anyplace in between, if your school is like most other schools it probably has its very own collection of cliques.

A COMMON GROUND

When you hear the word clique, does a little alarm go off in your head? Do you immediately conjure up all sorts of negative images? Many people do. Yet, aside from all the bad stuff that comes along with cliques, there is a positive side to the story as well. When you understand that, then you'll understand why cliques exist in the first place.

It's natural to want to be around people who think the way you do and share your interests. Think about the "jocks" or whatever they're labeled at your school. Maybe some of them are on school sports teams and others just have an interest in athletics of all kinds. Either way, sports in some shape or form are important to them. It makes sense that they like hanging out with other students who enjoy the same things.

Here's another example: the kids who are super-smart, the ones who study a lot and get good grades all the time. These students probably feel more comfortable with other people who give academics top priority. At their best, cliques are groups of friends who pursue common goals and share common interests.

TOO CLOSED FOR COMFORT

When do cliques present a problem? When the people in them keep themselves separate and exclude anyone who doesn't fit neatly into the image the group wants to project.

Here's a dictionary definition of a clique: "A narrow, exclusive group or circle of people, especially one held together by common interests, views, or purposes." The words *narrow* and *exclusive* are what most people think of when they think about cliques, and they're at the root of the problems cliques can create.

When cliques become too narrow and exclusive, they cause harm. Any time those "inside" a clique close themselves off to anyone "outside," you've got real trouble. Unfortunately, this happens all too frequently.

Imagine how you'd feel if a certain group of people didn't welcome you: confused, angry, embarrassed, hurt—in short, rejected. But let's turn the tables for a second. Can you think of a time when *you* were part of a clique that froze out a newcomer? How did that make you feel—about the clique, and about yourself? Perhaps you experienced some of the same feelings as the person who was kept out of the clique. You might have felt *embarrassed* to be part of a group that did such a mean thing. You might have been *angry* at yourself for having allowed the "freeze-out" to happen. You might have been *confused* about why you went along with the group's decision. Finally, if you're the kind of person who hurts when someone else is hurt, then you also felt this person's *pain* at being rejected.

Was the person your clique froze out someone you might have really liked? You'll never know, because you froze out your chance for friendship with him or her.

A closed clique can be extremely stifling to its members. Often, the result is missed opportunities for friendship. Many people are so intimidated by the strength some cliques seem to wield that they don't even try to befriend any of the people in them.

But those who barricade themselves behind the walls of cliques aren't necessarily stronger for doing so. They don't just keep "intruders" out; they also keep themselves isolated from new ideas, new interests and new friendships. In the end, they're the ones who lose out.

☆☆ THE CLIQUE QUIZ ☆☆

Still not sure whether or not the group you're in constitutes a closed clique? Take the following quiz and find out.

1. *The people I hang out with:*
   a. All have other friends outside our group.
   b. Only hang out with each other.
2. *If my group of friends knew I liked a boy in another group:*
   a. They'd think that was okay.
   b. They'd say, "He's not one of us," and let me know that I was making a big mistake.
3. *The people in my group share:*
   a. Some of the same interests, and have others that are different.
   b. The exact same interests only.
4. *If I don't feel comfortable doing something my group plans to do:*
   a. They understand.
   b. They pressure me to the point that I feel I have to go along with them.
5. *If I meet someone I think is nice, and want to include*

her in some of my group's activities, my friends would:

    a. Say, "Great. When do we get to meet her?"

    b. Tell me it probably wasn't a good idea to bring her along.

Answers: If you answered "a" to more than two of the questions above, your clique doesn't close out others—or close you in. It's obvious that you've chosen your friends with care. If, on the other hand, you chose "b" more often than "a", take another look at your group. Use your own good judgment to decide if they aren't just a little too quick to judge others.

☆☆☆

BARRIERS TO BEWARE OF

How much money a person's family has—or doesn't have—can be one reason a clique might keep someone out. But, as I'm sure you know, economic background has nothing to do with whether two people like each other, and it certainly shouldn't be a barrier to friendship.

There are other things that should never act as friendship barriers, but sometimes do. Wouldn't you be hurt and angry if people didn't want you as a friend because of the color of your skin, a physical condition you had or the religion you belonged to? Of course you would! But some people automatically reject people just for those reasons. It's a situation where everybody loses—the person who's rejected isn't given a chance to show what he or she is really like, and the group misses out on getting to know someone who could become a good friend.

What does all this have to do with cliques? A lot! Even if you would never discriminate against someone, being a part of a clique that does makes you just as guilty. Don't be afraid to speak up if your friends are keeping someone out of your crowd for reasons you think are unfair. You'll be doing the right thing, and you might even change a few minds, too.

THE WRONG CROWD

Phew! Finally! You can't believe it! You're one of *them*, the group you've always admired. You eat lunch with them. Hang out with them. Go where they go. Do what they do. How lucky you are! How good you feel! Or so you thought.

Soon the excitement wears off and reality sets in. The more things you do with this oh-so-right crowd, the more you realize how oh-so-wrong they are for you. They like to gossip about people. (You don't.) They cut class occasionally. (You don't.) They shoplift every now and then. (You don't.)

So now what do you do? One thing you know for sure is that now that you're finally *in*, all you can think about is getting *out*.

How do you know if you're in the wrong crowd? Sometimes it's more obvious than others. If your new group of friends thinks shoplifting is fun, that's a clear-cut case of "wrong-crowd-itis." Actually, any time a group of friends says something illegal is okay, you know that *they* aren't the right crowd for you. Kids who are unkind to others are also people you should stay away from. If you're at all uncomfortable with what a group of people says or does, it's not the one for you.

But sometimes you can't help but notice a clique that seems to "have it all." Maybe the kids are popular. Maybe they're attractive. Maybe they just seem to have lots of fun together. You dream about how great it would be to have them as friends. Unfortunately, you can't always tell from the outside what things are really like on the inside.

Maybe you know kids who go along with the crowd even though they don't really want to because they're afraid that if they don't, they'll be teased or left out. They want to be "one of the gang," even if it means going against their own beliefs about what's right and what's wrong.

Once more, the self-esteem issue comes up. The higher your self-esteem, the more you'll realize that you don't have to do anything you don't want to do. You have a responsibility to yourself and your values. And any friend who tries to force you into a situation that you know is wrong or dangerous is no friend of yours.

UNFRIENDLY FRIENDS

You've probably heard the saying, "With friends like that, who needs enemies?" Well, the wrong crowd can also be a group of friends who simply don't treat you the way friends should. Tracy said she was once part of an unfriendly group of friends.

"We'd been 'friends' for a while," Tracy remembered, "but I never got the feeling that I was really one of them. I always had to make the first move to get together with them. Only once in a while did *they* call *me*. Sometimes I found out that they'd made plans, and everyone else but me was invited. One of the worst things that happened was that one of the girls told a guy I liked these terrible things about me— things that weren't true at all. That did it. I finally realized that no matter how popular they were, these girls weren't the kind of friends I wanted."

GETTING OUT

So what do you do if you find yourself in with the wrong group of friends? First, don't blame yourself and say, "How could I have let this happen?" It's not always easy to tell what people are really like until you get to know them. Still, once you are in, the idea of getting out can seem pretty scary.

How do you maneuver the big break? Your strategy may depend on *how* wrong your crowd is and how uncomfortable you actually feel being a part of it.

If you think your crowd is headed for serious trouble (cutting classes, shoplifting, taking drugs, drinking alcohol or doing anything else illegal), and could bring you down with them:

- ✪ *Don't wait until it's too late.* Better to get out immediately. If you have just one good friend outside the crowd, that's enough to help you through the tough times ahead. Even if you don't, it's better to go it alone for a while rather than risk a potential disaster. It won't be fun at first, but with a little effort you're sure to meet people who can be *real* friends.

○ *After you've broken off with them, don't accept invitations from them again.* Make excuses if you have to. If you're lonely, you may be eager to join them, but in the long run you'll be glad you didn't.

○ *Talk to an adult you trust.* That might be a parent, a school counselor or a teacher, but whoever it is, let her or him know what's going on. She or he may have some helpful ideas about how to handle this situation. It's always good to know that someone you trust is in your corner.

If nothing serious is wrong with the crowd, and if you like some of the people, but have decided that most of them just aren't right for you:

○ *You may be able to ease your way out.* Before you make a break, try to develop stronger friendships with the people in the group you *do* like.

○ *Get to know some new people.* Now's not the time to be shy. Ask that nice girl in your math class, and maybe the girl whose locker is next to yours, if they'd like to eat lunch with you. It's a step in the right direction.

○ *Call your "old" friends.* Now's the time to reconnect with people you've always liked, but haven't spent much time with lately.

Breaking away from the "wrong" clique gives you the freedom to make true friends.

What's the best way to avoid getting into the wrong crowd? When you *do* choose new friends, get to know them gradually. Pay attention to the way they act when they're together. Do they talk about each other kindly? Do they treat each other with respect? If you sense that something isn't right, better give your new group some serious second thoughts.

And, just because you think your new crowd will bring you instant star status at your school, don't toss aside former friends like an old pair of jeans because, like those well-worn jeans, old friendships are often the most comfortable.

Boys! Boys! Boys!

No book on friendship for girls would be complete without a section on—what else?—boys. Boys are likely to be a favorite subject for you and your friends, one you could probably spend hours discussing. Throughout the previous chapters, your friends—past, present and future—have been primarily referred to as female. Most of your friends may in fact be girls. Still, that doesn't rule out the possibility that some of them are boys.

And then, all of a sudden, someone who was once just a boy friend may become a potential boyfriend.

At about this same time you start trying to explain certain things to your girl friends. Maybe you've had a conversation that went something like this:

You say: "I like him."

They say: "What do you mean? Do you like him, or *like* him?"

You say: "I don't know. Right now, I think I just like him. Then again, I could really *like* him."

No matter how bowled over you are by boys in general, don't make the mistake of ruling them out as friends. When girls start seeing boys *only* as prospective dates they often forget how to be "just friends" with any boy. That's too bad, for a couple of reasons. First, a girl who doesn't know how to befriend a boy and only flirts probably wouldn't be the greatest girlfriend anyway. Friendship is an important part of any relationship—romance included. More important, though, boys can be really good friends.

"A boy who's your friend can be like a big brother," observed Megan. "The best part is that because he's really not your brother, you get along much better. There's no sibling rivalry. Plus, it's sometimes nice to hear things from the boy's point of view."

Boys can offer you a different perspective on things. And what girl wouldn't love to get the inside scoop on how the male mind operates? A boy who's your friend also may help you see your girl-friendships more clearly. Since he's obviously more removed from the situation than you are he can give you a more objective opinion. In addition, when you get used to talking with boys in general, some of the mystery that surrounds them wears off, and this can help you to feel more at ease with a boy you fall for later.

WHEN YOUR BEST FRIEND IS A BOY

If a boy can be your friend, can he also turn out to be your best friend? Why not? Who's to say that your personality and interests will necessarily match up better with someone just because she's a girl?

Take Marcia, for instance. She has more girl friends than she can count, but it's Richard who's her best friend.

"When we met, Richard and I just got along so well," explained Marcia. "It wasn't a boyfriend-girlfriend thing. We just liked a lot of the same stuff. I play soccer and so does he. We both love shopping at flea markets and secondhand stores. We're both movie fanatics. Most of all, I really like talking with Richard because I can tell him anything."

Are there ever any drawbacks to a boy-girl best friendship? "Some of my girl friends thought it was weird at first," Marcia admitted. "I guess they assumed that girls should naturally want to have other girls as best friends. Actually, I think they were a little jealous. Not everyone is lucky enough to have a friend—boy or girl—like Richard."

What should you do if your best friend is a boy and some of your girl friends react the way Marcia's did? As long as you make them feel secure about their friendship with you, the problem will probably disappear on its own.

HOW TO TALK TO BOYS

Ask yourself this question: What is it that makes the difference between your feelings about a guy who's "just a friend" and your feelings about a guy you really fall for? It's the same thing that makes it so different (and so much easier) to *talk to* a guy who's "just a friend." Because you're not worried about impressing him, you're more comfortable being yourself.

If one thing's bound to make you a bundle of nerves around a boy you like, it's the feeling that you *can't* be yourself. And for those who lack self-confidence, being themselves is a big problem. Again, the issue of self-esteem pops up. (It pops up a lot, doesn't it?) Just remember, it's a lot easier to convince someone else that you're likable if you like yourself.

Feeling good about yourself is definitely a plus when you want to have a conversation with a boy. But sometimes it might seem as if boys are alien creatures from another planet. They use slang which you don't always understand. They laugh at things you don't think are funny. They do things that don't make sense to you. It's enough to make even the world's most confident girl feel at a loss for words!

In trying to figure out what makes boys tick, some girls have a tendency to lump them all into one generic pile: "Boys think this . . ." or "Boys like girls who . . ." But think about your friends and how different each one of them is. Girls don't all

Be yourself around boys—they make terrific pals!

think alike, or like the same things, so why should boys?

All boys are *not* the same. That's rule number one when it comes to understanding them. Sounds simple, but if you realize that there is no single basic set of "boy beliefs" or interests, you're on your way to better communication.

UNTYING YOUR TONGUE

When you're interested in someone, it's natural to be nervous around them—especially at first. You know how it is. All you can wonder is, "What in the world do I say?" No need to stammer. Simply say "Hi." Then listen, *really* listen, to what he says. If you're trying to think of some clever quip, how can you possibly pay attention to his comments? Focusing on what *he* says is the best way to calm yourself down.

GETTING BEYOND SPORTS, CARS AND COMPUTERS

Maybe you sense that beneath his tough-guy exterior, or his shy-but-sweet smile, this guy is someone you'd like to get to know. But how do you find out what he's *really* like? This is a question every girl asks herself sooner or later. Try the following tactics:

✪ *Remember Rule No. 1: All boys are not the same.* Now that you know that boys' interests extend beyond sports, cars and computers, the trick is to find out what interests him.

✪ *Do some behind-the-scenes detective work.* What clubs is he involved in? Does he hang out with

62

a large group or with a smaller circle of close friends? Observe what those people are like. This will give you a clue about where and with whom he feels most comfortable. After you've done a thorough job of sleuthing, you'll have a better idea of what line of questioning to use on your subject.

✪ *Try talking to him one-on-one.* Lots of guys put on a different face when they're surrounded by their friends. While they're trying to impress you, they're also trying to impress their buddies. If you can spend some time with him alone, you'll automatically eliminate half the pressure. He'll feel more at ease, and you'll get a clearer picture of the "real" him.

✪ *Plan a time to talk when you're not likely to be interrupted.* When and where you have your first real face-to-face can have a lot to do with its success. Keep track of his schedule: when he gets to school, when he goes to his locker, when he's most likely to be alone. If you can catch him at one of those moments, he'll be less distracted and more likely to focus on you.

✪ *Don't interrogate, investigate.* When you finally do get him to yourself, even if it's just for a few minutes, ask him about something you know he'll want to talk about. You don't want to hurl a long list of questions at him. Instead, if he's planning the freshman fund-raising event, ask how it's going. If he's interested in drama, ask him if he's going to try out for the upcoming school play. He'll feel flattered you cared enough to notice.

✪ *Win his trust.* Both boys and girls reveal more

about themselves to people they trust. It's natural to feel frustrated if, after some time, you've only scratched the surface of a boy's personality. But don't forget that a guy usually has plenty of fears of his own and one of them just might be that you won't like him. The more he realizes that you like what you've seen so far, the more of himself he'll open up to you.

● *Be yourself.* Let's say you know he's a sports nut, but you're the type who shouts "Touchdown!" at a baseball game. Don't try to fake it or pretend to be someone you're not. It'll only get you into trouble later when the truth comes out. Besides, most guys can sense if a girl's interest isn't genuine. When neither of you can seem to get the words out quickly enough, you'll know you've hit on a subject that's really important to you both.

MORE THAN JUST A FRIEND

How do you let a boy know that not only do you like him, but you *like* him as well? Maybe he's a boy friend now, but you wish he were your *boyfriend.*

You may have tried all sorts of things to get the message across. You send your friends to find out from *his* friends how he feels about you. He asks *your* friends how they think you feel about him. But the one thing you usually *don't* do is tell him yourself how you feel.

It's a lot easier to find out how a person feels about you directly from that person. But many people have trouble expressing their feelings this way. If you can come straight out and tell your favorite guy that you've fallen for him, hooray for you! But if the mere thought of doing that frightens you beyond belief, here are some other ways that will help him get the hint:

- ✪ *The more interest you show in him, the more he'll know you're interested, so take the time to talk to him.*
- ✪ *Go out of your way to do something nice for him. For instance, if you notice that he seems down, write him a note that will cheer him up. If he does well on a test or at a game, send him a congratulations card.*
- ✪ *Do yourself a favor and forget trying to send your message through the grapevine. Sure, sometimes it works, but sometimes it doesn't. And when a third party gets involved, the message you want him to receive may get mixed up. He'd probably much rather find out how you feel from you!*

WHY DOES HE ACT SO WEIRD?

If a boy seems weird sometimes, it's because he's not always sure what to say to *you*. Even if he wants to impress you, he might have some pretty funny (and not-so-funny) ways of showing it. He'll tease you, throw things at you or pull your hair. He might even pretend to ignore you or act as if he doesn't like you at all when, in fact, he really does.

It's not always easy to figure out what a boy's strange behavior really means. Why not ask him directly? You don't want to say, "Why are you acting so weird?" That would only make him feel more

65

self-conscious than he already does. Instead, you might try a more subtle approach like, "I don't really understand what you meant when you said . . ." If he does like you, he'll probably be thrilled that you want to talk with him. With any luck, his answer will make more sense than his oddball behavior.

TWO FOR ONE?

Wonderful though they often are, boys can cause certain problems as well. What about when you and a friend like (as in *like*) the same guy? It could happen, you know. Sadly, many friendships have broken up because of a boy. If you and a girl friend find yourselves in competition for a guy, you both need to stop and think about it. Is he really worth a major blow-up? Is it worth losing a friend over him?

True, when you're in the clutches of a crush, the last thing you want to do is call it quits. So what do you do? Discuss the dilemma with your friend. It won't be easy, but if you communicate well, this should be a problem you can eventually work through. Crushes tend to come and go, but friendship can last a lifetime.

Friendship Fix-Its

What's the deal? One second, you and your friend are getting along great, then— WHAM!—just like that, something happens that makes you want to tear your hair out. She's mad. You're mad. She's sad. You're sad. It's at times like these you stop and say to yourself, "And I thought friendship was supposed to be fun."

Maybe you've also wondered why your friends— those same people who bring you so much happiness—can also cause you pain, aggravation and confusion. Don't worry; it's a question that boggles the minds of most girls your age. The answer is, if you didn't care about your friends so much, the problems between you wouldn't make you feel so bad. Just call it one of those necessary evils that often accompanies something good.

You're aware that you have high points and low points in your day, your week, your year and your life. Well, each friendship also goes through its own unique progression of lulls and surges, ups and downs. You may think that it's the "ups" in your friendship that keep it going. Well, it's true; without them, it probably wouldn't last. Just as important, though, is how you and your friend navigate through the stormier moments of your friendship. Sometimes, you have to realize that the only thing to do is to wait the "waves" out. Then again, if you can work your way through the bad times, the rest of your friendship will be all the stronger for it.

Making friends requires a certain amount of skill, and learning to keep those friendships from faltering is a true art. If you can spot a potential sticky situation coming, you'll have a head start in putting a stop to it. One way to do that is to check out some of the problems other girls have faced.

THE COLD SHOULDER

When Susan suddenly started getting the silent treatment from her friend, Eve, she knew something was up. "At first," said Susan, "I thought Eve was just sad about something, and that was why she was so quiet. I also thought that if she needed or wanted to talk to me, she would. But this behavior of hers went on for days, and she still wouldn't talk about what was wrong. That's when I got scared."

When a good friend starts treating you like the Invisible Woman, it's pretty obvious that the two of you have a problem. Getting her to tell you what that problem is may turn out to be the hardest part.

"I tried everything," said Susan. "Phone calls, letters, sending another friend as a messenger to ask what was wrong. Nothing worked. Finally, I followed Eve into the girls' bathroom at school, cornered her and said, 'Hey, I'm your friend and you've got me worried to death. What's wrong?' But it wasn't until she screamed back at me, 'You!' that I began to understand."

Until that moment, Susan had no idea that *she* was the reason for her friend's silence. It turned out that Eve had been sulking because she felt Susan was losing interest in their friendship. If Susan had known this in the first place, she would have been able to reassure Eve that nothing could have been further from the truth.

Even though a friend may turn away from you, or give you the cold shoulder, it's often a signal that she desperately needs to talk. At the same time, she may be so mad, hurt or confused that she's literally choked with emotion.

So, how do you get your "clam" to open up? You could try coaxing her out of her shell gently, but actually the more direct you are, the better your chances. Just keep at it. In time, she'll probably stop resisting since deep down inside she's aching to tell you what's wrong.

IS *THREE* A CROWD?

The dreaded threesome. How often have you heard the horror stories? Maybe you have two friends you really like, but whenever the three of you get together, the sparks start to fly.

Actually, three doesn't have to be a crowd. In fact, it's a number that can add up to one fun friendship. It all depends on how the three of you interact. A group of three friends is most awkward when two people are especially close. Then the third person feels left out. That's how Ann felt whenever she got together with Claire and Judy.

"If Claire and Judy were talking about something they'd done together without me," said Ann, "I'd feel stupid, like I had nothing to add to their conversation."

Two friends who haven't included another friend in their plans can make her feel better by going out of their way to explain that they didn't really mean to shut her out. In the future, they could try to be a little more sensitive to how she feels.

In a different threesome combination, two friends might be fighting for the third person's attention. That's when things can get nasty. And it's up to friend number three to take some action. If you're in that position, try to draw attention away from yourself. Suggest activities that all three of you can enjoy, such as a movie. And always try to involve both your friends in conversations, taking care not to leave one of them out.

A threesome can work wonders when two friends

A threesome can be twice as much fun as a twosome.

can't take each other in large doses. Jane, for example, has a friend, Leslie, whom she likes a lot—a little at a time. When they're around each other too long, Jane finds Leslie annoying. Leslie has a friend, Teresa, whom Jane also likes. Somehow, when Jane, Leslie *and* Teresa are together, everyone gets along beautifully.

"Teresa has a really good sense of humor," said Jane, "and she balances out Leslie's tendency to be so serious. None of us have ever been super-close, but this has made us closer."

THE POSSESSIVE PAL

If you have a friend who's possessive, you don't need anyone to tell you that it can be a real pain. Whenever you go to open your locker, she's already there to greet you. Whenever the phone rings, you just know that she's on the line. If you want to eat lunch with another friend, she insists that you eat with her. In fact, whenever you make plans with anyone else, she acts as if you've banished her to Siberia!

A possessive friend wants your friendship exclusively for herself. She obviously cares a lot about you, and that can be flattering. But if she practically keeps you prisoner, she's not considering you—only herself. Pretty soon, you start to think of your formerly fine friend as a pain.

Gretchen knows the problem of the possessiveness game all too well. When one of her best buddies decided to declare a monopoly on Gretchen's friendship, it nearly drove her crazy.

"Carla and I used to do lots together and we had fun. But then I *had* to be with her—all the time," Gretchen remembered. "I couldn't even go with another friend to a movie. If I did, she'd get really mad."

Even worse, Carla demanded Gretchen's undivided attention. She couldn't understand that Gretchen needed other friends, too. If Gretchen did invite several kids over to her house, Carla would go into another room and sulk until Gretchen came in. Then she would complain that Gretchen was ignoring her.

"We'd been friends for a few years before the possessiveness started," explained Gretchen. "I didn't want to hurt her, so at first I'd always go along with what she wanted. After a while, it wasn't fun anymore."

Because Carla kept such close tabs on her, Gretchen didn't have a chance to meet many new people. When she couldn't take it anymore, Gretchen got up the nerve to tell Carla, "You are my best friend but I want to be with other people, too."

Remember that a possessive friend probably feels insecure. When she has to share you with other people she sees it as a threat to the special bond the two of you share. In a case like this, it's best to tell her that she's not only hurting you, she's hurting your friendship. Emphasize that the two of you are really good friends and that you want to keep it that way. If you can help her to see that your friendship won't peter out just because the two of you spend some time apart, she may feel secure enough to put her possessiveness in the past.

THE TWO-FACED FRIEND

A two-faced friend—someone who says one thing to your face, and another thing behind your back—can spell double trouble for your friendship. First, she makes it difficult for you to trust her again. Second, after she's pulled such a mean trick, you're not sure you even want to.

Jessica and Sharon had gone through most of their friendship without too much turmoil—*until* Sharon found out that Jessica had made some hurtful statements about her to Kelly, one of their mutual friends.

"Jessica had always been nice to me," Sharon recalled, "and I never would have imagined that she could be so two-faced. But then I found out that she had told Kelly that I was a spoiled brat. I couldn't believe it at first. But when a couple of our other friends confirmed it, I knew I had to confront her.

"I said to Jessica, 'I've heard that you said something about me behind my back. Is it true?' She tried to get out of answering my question. I kept at it, though, and she finally admitted that maybe she had said some 'not-so-nice' things."

Sharon asked Jessica *why* she'd said what she did. "Jessica explained it like this: She said she was upset because Kelly was spending more time with me than with her."

But Sharon couldn't understand how, if Jessica really valued their friendship, she could damage it so easily. And her badmouthing not only hurt

74

Sharon's feelings: It made Kelly wonder if Jessica would do the same to her one day.

Instead of risking her friendship with both Kelly and Sharon, Jessica would have been much better off if she had gone directly to the other girls, and explained why she was upset. "Now Jessica and I are just *polite* friends, not close at all," said Sharon. "I lost a lot of faith in her."

Is it possible to undo the damage of this friendship dilemma? Can you ever be good friends with a friend who tried to stab you in the back?

"Maybe," said Sharon. "But only if your friend is able to convince you that you can trust her again, and that can take a *really* long time."

If you ever have to deal with a two-faced friend, Sharon's method is a good one to follow. First, though, make sure your sources are reliable. You'd hate to accuse your friend of something she didn't do.

If your friend repeatedly denies it, you have a choice. You can tell her that because she's your friend, you believe what she says. You should add that if she ever does have a complaint, she should tell you herself. You're letting her off the hook and you're also giving her a chance to prevent the problem from happening again.

On the other hand, if you're convinced that your friend would do the same thing all over again, your other option is to end the friendship. But that's a mighty big step. If you can get to the root of the problem, the two of you may be able to work out a solution.

TAKING THE TIME TO TALK

One thing can help keep misunderstandings to a minimum: talking things through. It's always better to head off problems before they get too big to control.

Still, telling your friend that you feel she's been acting like a louse lately isn't something you look forward to. It's never easy to tell someone you're upset. Here are a few tips to help make that heart-to-heart a little easier:

- ✪ *Talk it out* immediately. *If you let anger build up inside, then when you finally do let it out you might explode. Begin by telling your friend how much you like her, and let her know how much her friendship means to you.*
- ✪ *Don't make personal problems between you and your friend a public matter. Have your talk in a private place.*
- ✪ *Don't accuse your friend of anything before you've heard her side of the story. Give your viewpoint, then listen without interrupting as she gives hers.*
- ✪ *Use tact. No one likes to be told bluntly that they've done something wrong.*
- ✪ *Try to have an open mind. Don't always assume that you're right about everything. Remember, different people see things differently.*
- ✪ *Balance your negative comments with some positive ones. You'll soften the blow. Again, you can't possibly reaffirm enough that your friendship matters to you very much.*

Neither you nor your friend should expect your problems to disappear overnight. Understanding each other better should be your immediate goal. Once you do, you can start to work things out between you.

Can you put an end to friendship foul-ups for good? Probably not. But if you always keep the lines of communication open, you and your friend will have fewer problems and more fun!

IT'S HARD TO SAY YOU'RE SORRY

No one is perfect, not even your best friends. We all make mistakes, and being able to *apologize* and to *forgive* is essential for any friendship. Some people feel that the only way to forgive a person completely is to *forget* what she or he did, but that's not necessarily so. How else do we learn from our (or another person's) mistakes if we don't remember them?

WHEN TO LET A FRIENDSHIP GO

But what if a solution is nowhere in sight? What if you feel that your friendship has had too many foul-ups, and that it's fast approaching the point of no return? Do you keep hanging in there, hoping something will change?

Again, you're the only one who can decide what's right for you. Some "hurts" hurt so much that we think we'll never fully recover from them. In other cases, the pain fades with time. Remember, though, no friendship should give you more pain than pleasure.

When is a good time to get out? When your friend no longer makes you feel good about yourself. When you no longer feel good about her. When you feel worse being with her than being without her. These are all signs that your friendship is experiencing more than just a temporary slump.

If you decide that a friend doesn't make you feel good anymore, it's best to level with her. This gives both of you one last chance to save the friendship, if you want. No matter what, it's a touchy and unpleasant situation to have to face. But if you don't, you'll just end up hurting each other more. Saying goodbye to a friend is hard, but if you're sure you'll both be happier in the long run, it's the best move you can make.

When You're the New Kid in Town

Katie is one of those lucky girls. You know, the kind who seems to have everything. Brains, beauty, a great sense of humor and, as you might suspect, popularity plus. People—both young and old—enjoy being around her. If anyone was surrounded by faithful friends, it was Katie—until two years ago when Katie's secure world received a pretty strong jolt. Katie still remembers the day her mom dropped the bomb.

"I had just come home from swimming practice," recalls Katie. "We were getting ready for the All-County meet. In this really serious voice, Mom said she had something she wanted to talk to me about. When she announced that we were moving, I couldn't believe it. I just sat there, staring into space, too shocked to say anything."

ON THE MOVE

If you have ever had to move, then you can relate to what Katie was feeling. You're also not alone; millions of teens have "made a move" at one time or another, and some more than once. They survive, and if you've recently moved, are about to move or find out that you may do so in the future, rest assured you will survive, too. Just because you pack up your bags, you don't have to pack in your friendships.

There is a growing tendency in our faster-paced, ever-more-modern society for families to move not just once or twice, but sometimes three, four and five times. One of the biggest reasons? People change jobs more frequently than they used to. And when they change jobs, they often choose to move to a different city or state in order to advance their careers. Also, with women making up such a large part of the work force, many families now have not one, but *two* careers to manage: Dad's and Mom's. That can mean twice as many moves.

I'LL NEVER FIT IN

Katie had living proof all around her—her friends—that she was a well-liked person. Still, once her mom's words started to sink in, the first thought that came to Katie's mind was that she would never fit in. A new city, hundreds of miles away, seemed to Katie like a foreign country. She wouldn't know her way around. She wouldn't know what "language" the kids there spoke. She wouldn't know if her clothes would be the right ones, or if her hair style was "in." Worst of all, she wouldn't know anybody.

All of this, of course, gave Katie a whopping case of the "what-am-I-going-to-dos." Imagine if you found out that you were going to be in Katie's shoes—that your family would be moving far from where you now live. What would worry you most? After reading the following list, write down the number of each item that would make you anxious about moving:

1. Leaving my old friends behind.
2. Being lonely because I won't know anyone.
3. Feeling like I'll always be "new."
4. Wondering if my new friendships will measure up to my old ones.
5. Questioning whether I'll measure up; will *they* like *me*?
6. Feeling like I'll never fit in.

By any chance, did you happen to check off every single one? If so, you're perfectly normal. These are fears that most people have about moving. Your parents may also share some of the same feelings, even if they were the ones who decided on the move in the first place.

Knowing that your fears are normal, though, doesn't do much to make them easier to deal with. What will really help is exploring why you have them and, finally, what you can do to conquer them.

LEAVING OLD FRIENDS BEHIND

Just because you move, it doesn't mean that your old friends will disappear from your life. In fact, friends that are forced to separate often develop a special bond. It's the old absence-makes-the-heart-grow-fonder theory. Nonetheless, it's natural to find that you miss your old friends—lots.

"When I moved, I cried for days," remembers Wendy. "I missed my friends from home so much. Even the phone calls I made didn't seem to help much; sometimes they made me miss my friends even more. It took time, but once I started to meet people, I began to feel better. Even though I still missed my old friends, the new friends I made eventually helped to fill the emptiness."

No one's trying to downplay how much you will miss your old friends. But if you realize that this "missing" period will have an end to it, you'll also see that there is a bright light at the end of this tunnel. Here's a chance to make a new beginning— several of them. So take a look around. Feast your eyes. You have the opportunity to make a whole new batch of friendships.

INITIAL LONELINESS

It makes sense that if you move to a place where you don't know a single soul, you'll probably be more than a little lonely. You might also feel isolated and a little lost. These are not the greatest feelings. True, some people don't seem to mind being alone and all of us need time to ourselves every now and then. But most people prefer to be around others. It's simply human nature to want company.

When you show up at your new school the first day and don't recognize a single face in the crowd, you will undoubtedly be lonely. This can be quite an overwhelming feeling, especially if you think you're going to feel this way forever. You won't. Loneliness often encourages people to make more of an effort to find new friends. By coaxing you out of your shell, your loneliness will have worked to your advantage—and guess what? You won't be lonely much longer.

NEW NOW, BUT NOT FOREVER

Try thinking back to the last time a new student walked into one of your classes. Maybe it was several months ago. Your teacher probably introduced the new person. Now, think of that same person right now. Do you still think of her or him as "new"? Probably not. You just think of that person like any other student. You might even have forgotten that he or she was *ever* new.

Some young people who learn that they will be moving fear that they'll be labeled NEW forever. This is simply not true. When you're new in school, you're also self-conscious about it, but you probably think about it a lot more than anyone else. Sure, in the beginning people will notice that you're new. But the longer you're there, the more they'll take you for granted.

FITTING IN

What can you do to feel more comfortable? Get involved in activities you enjoy. Anything you do—from playing a sport to trying out for the school play—will help you to forget about being new. You're bound to find your niche if you give it some effort, and you'll meet a bunch of interesting people in the process.

The other thing to remember is that people are always curious about newcomers. That's why a new student in school is often a hot topic of conversation. "I remember when Sandy, who's now my best friend, first came to my school," said Erin. "My friends and I were all wondering what she was like, if she was nice, if she'd be somebody to be friends with. That made us want to get to know her—and I'm sure glad I did!"

GREAT EXPECTATIONS

Many girls who face a move worry that even if they do manage to make friends, they won't be able

Trying out for the school play is a great way to make friends when you move to a new town.

to form the kinds of friendships they had back home. They're afraid the friendships won't be as special or that the new people they meet won't measure up to their old friends.

Teens and pre-teens who have these fears place an unfair burden on their friends-to-be, as well as on themselves. First of all, no two friendships are the same. Also, if a friendship is going to have a chance to succeed, it helps to give it the benefit of the doubt. In other words, if you start a new friendship expecting that it won't be as good as your old friendships, it probably won't. Your own expectations and attitudes often determine what kind of people—and friendships—you will find. If you arrive at your new school convinced that no one could possibly be as wonderful as your old friends, it's doubtful that you'll ever find anyone who is. Some wonderful people could be sitting right under your nose and you wouldn't even know it. Once you make up your mind that friends—fantastic friends—can be found anywhere, you'll be on your way to finding more than a few.

WILL I MEASURE UP?

This is, quite possibly, the number-one worry that haunts anyone who moves to a new place. Even Katie, who had a whole flock of friends, had this fear. Her own friends knew her and liked her. But at her new school Katie felt she had to prove herself. Would these people laugh at her jokes? Katie's old friends had, no matter how awful the jokes had been. Would they understand that Katie cried at the drop of a hat—whether she was happy or sad—or would they make fun of her? In short, Katie wondered if these strangers would like her for who she was.

This dilemma forced Katie to ask herself some tough questions. Did *she* like herself? Did she feel good about who she was? Would she want to be her own friend? How about you? How would you answer the same kind of questions that Katie asked herself? Well, here's your chance to find out. Take some time to read over and think about the following questions, then write your responses on a piece of notebook paper:

GETTING TO KNOW YOU

1. *Do you like yourself?*
   a. Yes   b. No   c. Not sure
2. *List at least three things that make you feel good about who you are.*
3. *Name three things about yourself that you wish you felt better about.*
4. *If you met someone exactly like you, would you want to be that person's friend? Why or why not?*

Why ask yourself all these questions? To start, if you want other people to like you, it helps tremendously if you like yourself. If there are certain things you don't like about yourself, ask whether you'd mind those same things as much in someone else. Usually we're much harder on ourselves than other people would be.

If there is an area that you feel needs improvement (for example, maybe it bothers you that you have a terrible temper), pinpointing the problem will allow you to work on it. Finally, when you learn to believe in yourself and realize that you *are* somebody special, you'll have a much easier time convincing others that you've got something special to contribute to a friendship.

Katie found that basically she liked the answers she got. Although she knew she could work on one or two fine points, in general, she felt she was a person whom she herself would like to befriend. Armed with this self-confidence, she made lots of new friends at her new school and pretty soon her fears were forgotten.

HOW TO FIT IN—AND STILL BE YOU

You may still be plagued by one nagging question. This one can come at you whether you move to a different country, move down the block or stay put: How can you fit in and still be you?

Truthfully, the best way to fit in is to be yourself. People like people who aren't afraid to be themselves. You can probably sense when someone is being phony or insincere. Take, for example, the people who seem to agree with you on everything. Doesn't that bug you? It's as if they don't have minds of their own. Worst of all, you never know what they really *do* think. What kind of a foundation for friendship is that?

Then why do so many people find it a challenge to be themselves? You'd think that nothing would be easier. But an undeniable connection exists between belief in yourself and being yourself. Feeling good about who you actually are gives you the strength and the freedom to be yourself. We're back to the issue of self-esteem again.

Does this mean that if you learn to accept yourself you'll worry less about what other people think of you? Eventually yes, but maybe not right away. Most people worry to some extent about what other people think of them. And who are we kidding? Everybody needs a healthy dose of approval every now and then.

The trick is to get the major share of that approval from yourself. When you can learn to do that, being yourself becomes second nature, because when you feel comfortable with who you are, not only will other people respect you, but *you* will respect you. When it comes to forming new friendships, what could be more important?

Friendship from Afar

What if you're not the one who has to move? What if one of your friends—maybe even your best friend—announces that she will be moving, maybe not clear across the country but far enough to make it seem that way?

It happened to Jill and Emily. Best friends since shortly after their birth (they were even born in the same hospital), Jill and Emily had gone to preschool, kindergarten, grade school and, finally, junior high school together. Through it all, they had kept their friendship alive and well. Sure, there had been moments when the two got on each other's nerves, but all in all, neither could have asked for a better friend.

The girls were looking forward to spending the summer together when they got the news. Jill came to school with her eyes red and puffy, and Emily immediately knew that something was wrong.

Between sobs, Jill managed to sputter out the horrible thing she had heard an hour earlier: "I'm moving! What are we going to do?"

Both Emily and Jill felt as if the wind had been knocked out of them. Jill's family was moving too far away for the girls to see each other often. If they were lucky, they'd be able to visit during vacations and summers. It took weeks for the shock to wear off and for reality to set in. But in crying and talking together about the move, Jill and Emily resolved that they were not going to let this long-distance road-block stand in the way of their friendship. And it hasn't.

CHANGING EXPECTATIONS

As they discussed the impending move, Jill and Emily found that what scared them the most was the idea of their being apart. Not only had they gone to the same school their whole lives, they had lived within walking distance from each other. Jill spent almost as much time at Emily's house as she did at her own. Yes, they each had other friends, but for Jill, there was no friend as close as Emily, and for Emily, there was no one like Jill. How could their friendship ever be the same?

Actually, it couldn't be exactly the same. Still, it took a while (as well as a few talks with their parents) for Jill and Emily to understand and accept that.

Obviously, if someone you spent so much time with was suddenly not part of your everyday picture, things would seem more than a little off balance. You'd feel like something wasn't quite right. Your life would seem different—and difficult—because of this change. To make matters worse, the person you had always counted on to make you feel better at such times wasn't going to be right around the corner anymore.

No doubt about it: Separation is no fun. But it won't hurt so badly forever. When you go to sleep every night praying that your friend's family will discover what a terrible mistake they've made and move back, it's hard to believe that you'll ever get over her absence. But you will, and here's one thought that might help you to rest more easily: Just remember that she misses you just as much as you miss her.

What else can help make a long-distance friendship more tolerable? Realizing that no matter how far away your friend is, you haven't "lost" her; she's still your friend. But you and she will have to alter your expectations. You can't expect your friendship to operate in the same way, even though your feelings for each other haven't changed. What *will* change are the ways in which the two of you maintain your friendship and keep it going strong.

You might compare your new friendship status to a dress— a special dress that you pick out for a very special occasion. Because you don't wear it every day, you look forward to the moment you finally put it on. It's sort of the same with a long-distance friendship. Because you don't see your friend every day as you used to, you're excited when you talk to her on the phone, receive a letter from her and, best of all, when you get to visit her. You realize just how special she really is.

Also, although your friend isn't physically present on a regular basis, she can still be an anchor for you. When things go wrong, when everything in your life seems to be topsy-turvy, you know that there is somebody out there who cares about you. She cares about what's happening to you, she misses you and she's rooting for you. No, you can't reach out to her for a comforting hug—and that would sure be nice—but because she's in your thoughts and you know you're in hers, she's there for you.

One of the things that Emily and Jill found most frustrating about living far apart was that they couldn't share the same experiences they used to: gymnastics classes, eating at their favorite pizza place, talking about the cute guys they'd see in the mall when they went shopping together. But they found a way that they could "hang out" together, even though they were apart.

While they couldn't actually do things together, Jill and Emily could share their own individual experiences with each other in their letters. "I often found myself wondering what Emily would think of this or that," says Jill. "In a store, I'd ask myself, 'Would Em make me buy this blouse or would she say it was too expensive and that I should leave it on the rack?' When I'd see a movie I knew she would like, I'd imagine what Emily would say about it if she were sitting next to me in the theater. I finally started keeping track of these little thoughts and then I'd tell her everything when I wrote or talked to her next. She started doing the same thing, and it's a lot of fun."

Far-apart friends often report that it's as if they've learned to see things not just for themselves, but for the friend who's not there as well. This is just one of the ways you can keep your faraway friendship close to your heart.

THE SENDOFF

One of the best things you can do to get a long-distance friendship off to a good start is to let your friend who's moving know how much you'll miss her. You might think, "How silly; of course she knows I'm going to miss her." Yes, she probably does, but is that any reason to let something so important go unsaid?

One of the fears many people have about becoming long-distance friends is that their friendship won't last. What better reason to assure your friend who's moving that she means an awful lot to you and that you're not about to forget her?

Saying what you feel is a good place to start, although a simple "I'm going to miss you" may not be enough. If you can say *why* you're going to miss your friend, you'll be much more effective in getting your point across. Give concrete examples, such as, "I'm really going to miss the way you always make me laugh," or "I'm really going to miss our Saturday-night make-over sessions." You'll obviously tailor what you'll say to your own friendship, and that's what will make it extra special.

Want another nice way to say goodbye to your friend? Write her a special "friendship note." Many people feel they express their feelings more clearly in writing, and by doing so you give your friend something tangible to remind her of your friendship, something she can hold on to and take with her to her new home. Here are some of the things you might want to include in it:

What to Include in a Friendship Note

✪ *Your memories of the first time you met.*
✪ *Your early impressions of your friend. (Did you like her right away? Did you think she would want to be friends with you?)*
✪ *What things led to the deepening of your friendship?*
✪ *Describe one of the funniest moments you can recall from your friendship.*
✪ *Describe one of the times when you were feeling down and your friend cheered you up.*
✪ *What problems, if any, did the two of you have to work out?*
✪ *What special things will you miss most about her?*

Now, whenever your friend misses you, or is feeling lonely and worrying that she won't make friends at her new school, all she has to do is pick up your note and read. All the reassurance she needs will be right there in your handwriting.

If you really want to go all out, you might (with your parents' permission) throw your friend a going-away party. You could ask all the guests to

Giving a pal who's moving a friendship note reassures her that she'll be missed.

bring a small gift for the friend who's leaving. Need some ideas? How about:

- *An address book with the names, addresses, phone numbers and birthdays of all her friends.*
- *Some pretty stationery.*
- *A special going-away scrapbook, filled with photos of her friends, poems about friendship and so on.*
- *An item of clothing or an accessory that she liked to borrow—often—and that you wouldn't mind parting with.*

Remember, while a party lets your friend know how much you care about her, it's even more important that she hears it from you directly.

DON'T LET THE DISTANCE KEEP YOU APART

For any friendship to stay glued together, you've got to give it some effort. Even if circumstances limit that effort to phone calls, remembering each other's birthday and occasional get-togethers, without attention even the strongest friendship bonds can break.

For a friendship-across-the-miles to succeed, the kind of effort you make (or don't) will *definitely* make the difference in whether you and your friend stick together. That doesn't mean both of you should feel compelled to write to each other every day, but you will want to stay in touch on a regular basis. Sure, there will be times when you can't respond to a letter as quickly as you'd like, but don't let your friend think you've forgotten her completely.

Two friends, Valerie and Betsy, acknowledged that their dependable stream of contact has kept their long-distance friendship together for almost five years. They say there's an easy trick to this.

"Both of us have hectic schedules," says Valerie. "Studying, music lessons, sports . . . you name it. So we don't always have the time to sit down and write long letters. Instead, I'll often clip out a funny comic strip, and send it to Betsy, and she does the same thing. Or, if I'm thinking about trying a new hair style I saw in a magazine, I'll clip out the page and ask Betsy what she thinks. Something else we do is send pictures—lots of them. Postcards are another shortcut."

Valerie and Betsy have gotten the business of keeping in touch down to a science, and they point out that their so-called "shortcuts" haven't short-changed their friendship.

"This isn't meant to be an easy way out of letter writing," explained Betsy. "It's a way of keeping our friendship really alive—like we're not so far away. We still make time for one, maybe two good letters a month. And we're talking eight-pagers at *least*."

ALTERNATIVES TO TELEPHONE TIME

Valerie and Betsy may have filled you in on some secrets that make staying in touch quite simple. But by now, you might be thinking, "Isn't it simpler just to pick up the telephone?" Yes, it is, but it's also much more expensive.

Since telephone time can cost big-time bucks,

parents often monitor their phone bills carefully. So *before* you dial away, ask your parents how much phone time they'll allow you. If you approach it this way, rather than running up their phone bill and getting them angry, it could work to your advantage. They might even let you talk longer!

What else can you do to keep your long-distance friendship close? Lots of long-distance friends send each other letters on tape. Audio cassettes are easy to make and inexpensive to send, but if you're lucky enough to have a video camera, try that, too. Also, why not create a special friendship holiday? You could call it something like an "anniversary-of-our-friendship" day, in remembrance of the day you first met.

Use your imagination. You're sure to come up with a host of other ideas to further your friendship from afar.

NEW DOORS TO OPEN, NEW FRIENDS TO MEET

When one half of a twosome moves, both friends may feel like the road of their friendship has come to an end. Now you know that that doesn't have to be so. Emily and Jill, and Valerie and Betsy are just two of the terrific twosomes who have proved that, with a little direction, long-distance friendship *can* find a way.

Still, a move can make both people feel like a door has slammed shut. Though you might view a move as a crisis at first, it is also an opportunity for you to branch out and make new friends. Your long-distance friend will always be with you in spirit, but you need people you can communicate with and share things with on a day-to-day basis, as well.

For the one who stays behind, that might mean cultivating a closer relationship with somebody who's already your friend. If you're the one who moves, the special friendships with your old friends are a wonderful foundation and have shown you what to look for in forming new friendships.

You've Got a Friend

*D*o you recognize a potential friend when you see one? Could you pick her out of a crowd? Is there some special quality that stands out and makes you say, "Boy, I bet it'd be fun to be her friend?"

You certainly know which traits you find attractive in a friend, and which ones turn you off. You may prefer pals who are poised, polished and polite. Someone else may want buddies who are just a bit weird, wacky and one-of-a-kind.

Often, people (and not just young people) put together a profile of the "perfect" friend. They don't actually say to themselves, "My friend has got to be this, this and this." Rather, an idea develops in their minds, subconsciously, about who and what their friends should be. By not looking further than their prepackaged, preformed notions, many people fail to see that friendship can wear many faces, and that friends can be found in many places.

THE MANY FACES OF FRIENDSHIP

Sarah and Liza probably never would have met had it not been for Biology. Or maybe it was the frog. But, lo and behold, there they were, two girls who seemed to have nothing in common except for the fact that they were thrown together for a science experiment. Little did Sarah and Liza know that this pairing, which at the time appeared to be a total disaster, would turn out to be their good fortune.

Sarah, a no-nonsense, no-frills tomboy type, remembered her first impression of Liza this way: "She was all buttons and bows, flowers and frills— everything I can't stand. I didn't think she could possibly have a brain beneath all that beauty. Boy, was I wrong!"

Liza wasn't too pleased by what she saw in Sarah, either. "She looked like one of those 'I'm-too-busy-to-bother-with-how-I-look-besides-I-don't-care' kind of girls. I could never have imagined that she'd want to have anything to do with me or, for that matter, that I'd want to have anything to do with her. And I never in a million years would have imagined that we'd become such good friends."

For their experiment, Sarah and Liza had to spend

hours on end together in the school's science lab. At first, both girls were uncomfortable; neither one knew what to say to the other, so their conversation didn't drift too far from the frog. But little by little, the more time they spent together, the more each girl began to notice something about the other that she liked. Sarah saw that Liza's "smarts" rivaled her own and that Liza's jokes often had her in stitches. Liza, in turn, found that Sarah not only understood her need to succeed—especially when it came to school—but shared it.

As a result, Sarah and Liza's frog experiment was awarded the highest grade in their class and the girls decided that they'd remain lab partners for the rest of the semester. But something much more important had also happened: Sarah and Liza had become friends.

Sarah and Liza's friendship illustrates the truth of the cliché, "Don't judge a book by its cover." Very often, friends turn out to be the very people you might never envision yourself befriending—until you know them better.

FRIENDSHIP—AT ANY AGE

Friends come in a host of different shapes, sizes, colors—and ages. Most likely, the majority of your friends are the same age as you, or close to it. But just because you're entering or in your teens, your friendships don't have to be limited to teenagers.

Many girls your age tend to shy away from friendships with kids who are younger simply because they're afraid that hanging around with someone younger will make them seem less grown-up.

Who ever said maturity had anything to do with age? You probably know a few "kids" who are much more mature than some older teens.

As an example, let's say you met a girl who was younger than you and who shared your love of art. Both of you enjoy going to museums, spending the day sketching or wandering through galleries. Can you think of one good reason not to pursue her friendship? We can't.

Now what about grownups? Maybe your track coach is someone you admire and can talk to easily. Perhaps you feel a favorite teacher really understands you. These adults, and people like them, can be your friends. Nowhere does it say that there's an age limit to friendship. A friend is a friend, no matter how young or how old.

PARENTS AS FRIENDS

Is it possible that your parents can also be your friends? Of course it is. But it's important to understand that they will always be your parents, first and foremost.

In order for them to be good parents, they often have to make some not-so-popular decisions. That's part of their job. Maybe they give you a curfew that you'd rather not have. Or they decide you shouldn't date until you're sixteen—something else you're not too pleased about. Decisions like these, that parents have to make and kids have to take, often come between parents and their children. But it's important that parents do the *right* thing, not necessarily the thing that's going to make you happy.

Try to put yourself in your parents' shoes: Pretend

Doing "non-parenting" activities with your folks will help you build a real friendship with them.

for a moment that you had to baby-sit your younger sister. She tells you that she wants to go and ride her bike with her friends. The problem is, you know that the area where she wants to ride isn't safe. What do you do? Even if she begs and pleads and says you're a meanie if you don't let her go, you know you shouldn't, so you don't. You did the *right* thing, not the thing that would have won you brownie points for friendship.

Parents do what they do because they love you. It's as simple as that. If you think that parents who let their children do as they please have better relationships with their kids, think again. Sure, it might sound great, but if your parents didn't set any limits—if they let you come and go as you please, if they didn't bug you about your homework, if they didn't take an interest in who your friends were—you'd probably feel that they didn't really care about you.

So how can you and your parents be friends even if you don't see eye-to-eye most of the time? First, remember that friends disagree once in a while, too, but they work it out. Some of the strongest parent-daughter friendships have grown out of conflict.

"My mom and I never used to get along," admits Marla. "We'd argue about everything: what I wore, what I ate, how much I talked on the phone, how I spent my free time. We drove each other crazy. But through all that arguing we somehow found a way to communicate. I discovered that I can talk to her, and she'll listen, and she knows I'll listen to her, too. We still don't agree on lots of things, but that's okay. Once we could talk to each other, we found we had more in common than we realized. Now, she's the friend I confide in more than any other."

Many teens and pre-teens are so sure that their parents couldn't possibly understand what they're feeling that they don't even give them a chance. Your parents were your age once, believe it or not. But if you really want their friendship, you'll need to accept their primary role in your life: parents. Then give them the opportunity to be your friends as well.

PARENTS ARE PEOPLE, TOO

Approach your friendship with your parents the same way you would any new friendship:

1. *Get to know each other.* Even though you've lived together all these years, you may not really know what your parents are like as people. How did they choose their careers? What are their favorite hobbies? If they could take a year off from work, what would they do?

2. *Discover the things you have in common.* If you dig down deep enough, you're bound to find something you can share. Maybe your mom likes the same kinds of movies you do. Maybe you and your dad both enjoy the outdoors. Perhaps you all share an interest in environmental issues.

3. Friends don't leave their fun get-togethers up to chance; usually they plan them. So *schedule some positive, "non-parenting" time with your parents* (perhaps for one of the "common ground" activities you came up with earlier). They'll probably appreciate the break as much as you.

SIBLINGS AND ALL THAT "RELATIVE" STUFF

Your sister shows up at school in your favorite skirt. Your brother digs into your desk and finds

109

your diary. Endearing? Hardly. The only thing on your mind is how you're going to get revenge.

Like all teens and pre-teens, you probably get into your share of sibling spats. At times, you may have wished that your brother or sister belonged to someone else's family. When it gets right down to it, though, you wouldn't write them off as relatives, and you shouldn't rule them out as friends. This doesn't mean you and your siblings have to be close friends. But at least recognize that, as with any family member—grandparent, cousin, uncle, aunt— much of the framework for friendship is already in place.

Maybe you have a little brother who drives you up a wall most of the time. Still, if someone were to make fun of him, you'd come to his defense in an instant. That's because loyalty and love are part of any family relationship. With a head start like that, you'll find that family ties can foster first-rate friend-ships.

A LITTLE FRIENDSHIP CAN GO A LONG WAY

When can a stranger be a friend? When you "volunteer" your friendship to someone who could really use it.

So many people in the world aren't as lucky as you and your friends. They may be disabled, sick or simply less fortunate. Often, a friend is the very thing these people need to brighten up their lives.

It sounds so simple, but to an older person in a rest home, a child from a broken home or anyone who may be lonely, a little of your friendship can go a long way. Spending just a little time with people

110

like this—maybe even only an hour or two a week—is one of the nicest things you can do for them. It's also one of the nicest things you can do for yourself. The warm feeling you get from making someone else feel good can't be beat.

Think you might be interested in volunteering your friendship? Check around your school and community for clubs or service organizations. If they already have volunteer programs set up, all you'll need to do is sign up.

Finally, don't forget that any time you're *being* a friend, you're also *making* one.

QUALITY VS. QUANTITY

Who would you say scores higher on the friendship scale—a girl who has tons of friends or one who has a few who are very close? Well, that depends on your definition of friendship.

For some people, a friend is anyone they say a quick "hello" to in the school corridors. These people have *lots* of so-called friends. But an abundance of casual acquaintances isn't the same thing as having many friends.

People who surround themselves with a few good friends understand that what their friendships lack in quantity, they more than make up for in quality. For some girls, just having one great friend is enough.

"In my first year of junior high," said Sonya, "I hung out with lots of kids that other people might have called friends, but I didn't. Yeah, I went places and did things with some of them, but I never really felt that I could confide in them, be myself with them or even trust them. During that year, my friend Allison was the only person I would have called a real, honest-to-goodness friend. She was always there for me, and knowing that I could count on her made everything okay."

Does that mean that someone with many friends doesn't have any meaningful, valuable friendships? Of course not. It simply means that the *number* of friends you have (or don't have) has little or no bearing on the happiness you derive from those relationships. In friendship, what counts is closeness.

A Friend Is One Who Loves You

I n the first pages of this book, you were asked a question: Can you imagine what life would be like without friends?

Centuries ago, the philosopher Aristotle said that "without friends no one would choose to live." How's that for an answer?

You might have expected Aristotle to have said that without *love* no one would choose to live, but he didn't, and Aristotle, rest assured, was a man who chose his words quite carefully. Clearly he felt that friends are very, very important.

Aristotle probably knew that real friendship and real love cannot exist without each other. In other words, to be a true friend, you must love, and to truly love, you must also be a friend.

Where does love fit into your friendships? To answer that question, you don't have to look any further than the feelings you have for your own friends:

- ✪ *A friend is someone you enjoy being with, and who enjoys being with you, too. What could make you feel more* worthwhile?
- ✪ *A friend is someone you share constant discoveries with. What could make you feel more* alive?
- ✪ *A friend is someone you choose, and who, in turn, chooses you. What could make you feel more* special?

Worthwhile. Alive. Special. These are just a few of the feelings a friend brings out in you, and oh, what fabulous feelings they are!

For most of our lives, we all search high and low, looking for love, believing that love is what makes life worthwhile. But if a friend is one who loves you, then love is not hard to find. It is always within reach, wrapped up tidily in a simple but powerful little package called friendship.